Editor
Cristina Krysinski, M. Ed.

Editor in Chief
Karen J. Goldfluss, M.S. Ed.

Creative Director
Sarah M. Fournier

Cover Artist
Barbara Lorseyedi

Art Coordinator
Renée Mc Elwee

Imaging
Amanda R. Harter

Publisher
Mary D. Smith, M.S. Ed.

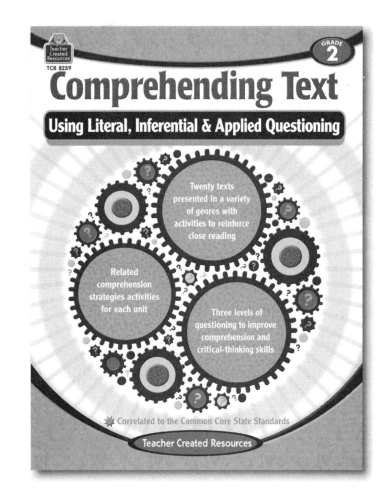

For correlations to the Common Core State Standards, see page 109 of this book or visit *http://www.teachercreated.com/standards*.

Teacher Created Resources
6421 Industry Way
Westminster, CA 92683
www.teachercreated.com
ISBN: 978-1-4206-8239-7

© *2015 Teacher Created Resou*
Made in U.S.A.

D0838854

Table of Contents

Introduction

Twenty different texts from a variety of genres are included in this reading comprehension resource. These may include humor, fantasy, myth/legend, folktale, mystery, adventure, suspense, fairy tale, play, fable, science fiction, poetry, and informational/nonfiction texts, such as a timetable, letter, report, procedure, poster, map, program, book cover, and cartoon.

Three levels of questions are used to indicate the reader's comprehension of each text.

One or more particular comprehension strategies have been chosen for practice with each text.

Each unit is five pages long and consists of the following resources and strategies:

- teacher information: includes the answer key and extension suggestions
- text page: text is presented on one full page
- activity page 1:   covers literal and inferential questions
- activity page 2:   covers applied questions
- applying strategies: focuses on a chosen comprehension strategy/strategies

Teacher Information

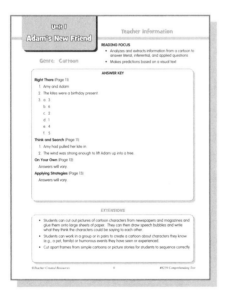

- **Reading Focus** states the comprehension skill emphasis for the unit.
- **Genre** is clearly indicated.
- **Answer Key** is provided. For certain questions, answers will vary, but suggested answers are given.
- **Extension Activities** suggest other authors or book titles. Other literacy activities relating to the text are suggested.

Text Page

- The title of the text is provided.
- Statement is included in regard to the genre.
- Text is presented on a full page.

Activity Page 1

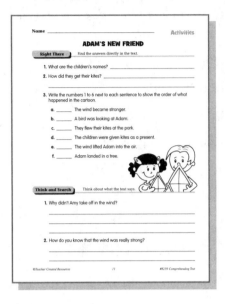

- **Right There** consists of literal questions.
- **Think and Search** consists of inferential questions.

Activity Page 2

- **On Your Own** consists of applied questions.

Applying Strategies

- Comprehension strategy focus is clearly labeled.
- Activities provide opportunities to utilize the particular strategy.

Types of Questions

Students are given **three types of questions** (all grouped accordingly) to assess their comprehension of a particular text in each genre:

- **Literal questions (Right There)** are questions for which answers can be found directly in the text.

- **Inferential questions (Think and Search)** are questions for which answers are implied in the text and require the reader to think a bit more deeply about what he or she has just read.

- **Applied questions (On Your Own)** are questions that require the reader to think even further about the text and incorporate personal experiences and knowledge to answer them.

Answers for literal questions are always given and may be found on the Teacher Information pages. Answers for inferential questions are given when appropriate. Applied questions are best checked by the teacher following, or in conjunction with, a class discussion.

Comprehension Strategies

Several specific comprehension strategies have been selected for practice in this book.

Although specific examples have been selected, often other strategies, such as scanning, are used in conjunction with those indicated, even though they may not be stated. Rarely does a reader use only a single strategy to comprehend a text.

Strategy Definitions

Predicting — Prediction involves the students using illustrations, text, or background knowledge to help them construct meaning. Students might predict what texts could be about, what could happen, or how characters could act or react. Prediction may occur before, during, and after reading, and it can be adjusted during reading.

Making Connections — Students comprehend texts by linking their prior knowledge with the new information from the text. Students may make connections between the text and themselves, between the new text and other texts previously read, and between the text and real-world experiences.

Comparing — This strategy is closely linked to the strategy of making connections. Students make comparisons by thinking more specifically about the similarities and differences between the connections being made.

Sensory Imaging — Sensory imaging involves students utilizing all five senses to create mental images of passages in the text. Students also use their personal experiences to create these images. The images may help students make predictions, form conclusions, interpret information, and remember details.

Strategy Definitions *(cont.)*

Determining Importance/ Identifying Main Idea(s)

The strategy of determining importance is particularly helpful when students try to comprehend informational texts. It involves students determining the important theme or main idea of particular paragraphs or passages.

As students become effective readers, they will constantly ask themselves what is most important in a phrase, sentence, paragraph, chapter, or whole text. To determine importance, students will need to use a variety of information, such as the purpose for reading, their knowledge of the topic, background experiences and beliefs, and understanding of the text format.

Skimming

Skimming is the strategy of looking quickly through texts to gain a general impression or overview of the content. Readers often use this strategy to quickly assess whether a text, or part of it, will meet their purpose. Because this book deals predominantly with comprehension after reading, skimming has not been included as one of the major strategies.

Scanning

Scanning is the strategy of quickly locating specific details, such as dates, places, or names, or those parts of the text that support a particular point of view. Scanning is often used, but not specifically mentioned, when used in conjunction with other strategies.

Synthesizing/Sequencing

Synthesizing is the strategy that enables students to collate a range of information in relation to the text. Students recall information, order details, and piece information together to make sense of the text. Synthesizing/sequencing helps students to monitor their understanding. Synthesizing involves connecting, comparing, determining importance, posing questions, and creating images.

Summarizing/Paraphrasing

Summarizing involves the processes of recording key ideas, main points, or the most important information from a text. Summarizing or paraphrasing reduces a larger piece of text to the most important details.

Genre Definitions

Fiction and Poetry

Science Fiction
These stories include backgrounds or plots based upon possible technology or inventions, experimental medicine, life in the future, environments drastically changed, alien races, space travel, genetic engineering, dimensional portals, or changed scientific principles. Science fiction encourages readers to suspend some of their disbelief and examine alternate possibilities.

Suspense
Stories of suspense aim to make the reader feel fear, disgust, or uncertainty. Many suspense stories have become classics. These include *Frankenstein* by Mary Shelley, *Dracula* by Bram Stoker, and *Dr. Jekyll and Mr. Hyde* by Robert Louis Stevenson.

Mystery
Stories from this genre focus on the solving of a mystery. Plots of mysteries often revolve around a crime. The hero must solve the mystery, overcoming unknown forces or enemies. Stories about detectives, police, private investigators, amateur sleuths, spies, thrillers, and courtroom dramas usually fall into this genre.

Fable
A fable is a short story that states a moral. Fables often use talking animals or animated objects as the main characters. The interaction of the animals or animated objects reveals general truths about human nature.

Fairy Tale
These tales are usually about elves, dragons, goblins, fairies, or magical beings and are often set in the distant past. Fairy tales usually begin with the phrase "Once upon a time . . ." and end with the words ". . . and they lived happily ever after." Charms, disguises, and talking animals may also appear in fairy tales.

Fantasy
A fantasy may be any text or story removed from reality. Stories may be set in nonexistent worlds, such as an elf kingdom, on another planet, or in alternate versions of the known world. The characters may not be human (dragons, trolls, etc.) or may be humans who interact with non-human characters.

Folktale
Stories that have been passed from one generation to the next by word of mouth rather than by written form are folktales. Folktales may include sayings, superstitions, social rituals, legends, or lore about the weather, animals, or plants.

Play
Plays are specific pieces of drama, usually enacted on a stage by actors dressed in makeup and appropriate costumes.

Genre Definitions (cont.)

Fiction and Poetry (cont.)

Adventure Exciting events and actions feature in these stories. Character development, themes, or symbolism are not as important as the actions or events in an adventure story.

Humor Humor involves characters or events that promote laughter, pleasure, or humor in the reader.

Poetry This genre utilizes rhythmic patterns of language. The patterns include meter (high- and low-stressed syllables), syllabication (the number of syllables in each line), rhyme, alliteration, or a combination of these. Poems often use figurative language.

Myth A myth explains a belief, practice, or natural phenomenon and usually involves gods, demons, or supernatural beings. A myth does not necessarily have a basis in fact or a natural explanation.

Legend Legends are told as though the events were actual historical events. Legends may or may not be based on an elaborated version of a historical event. Legends are usually about human beings, although gods may intervene in some way throughout the story.

Nonfiction

Report Reports are written documents describing the findings of an individual or group. They may take the form of a newspaper report, sports report, or police report, or a report about an animal, person, or object.

Letter These are written conversations sent from one person to another. Letters usually begin with a greeting, contain the information to be related, and conclude with a farewell signed by the sender.

Procedure Procedures tell how to make or do something. They use clear, concise language and command verbs. A list of materials required to complete the procedure is included, and the instructions are set out in easy-to-follow steps.

Other **informational texts**, such as **timetables**, **posters**, **programs**, and **maps**, are excellent sources to teach and assess comprehension skills. Highly visual texts, such as **book covers** and **cartoons**, have been included to provide the reader with other comprehension cues and are less reliant on word recognition.

Teacher Information

Genre: Cartoon

READING FOCUS

- Analyzes and extracts information from a cartoon to answer literal, inferential, and applied questions
- Makes predictions based on a visual text

ANSWER KEY

Right There (Page 11)

1. Amy and Adam

2. The kites were a birthday present.

3. a. 3

   b. 6

   c. 2

   d. 1

   e. 4

   f. 5

Think and Search (Page 11)

1. Amy had pulled her kite in.

2. The wind was strong enough to lift Adam up into a tree.

On Your Own (Page 12)

Answers will vary.

Applying Strategies (Page 13)

Answers will vary.

EXTENSIONS

- Students can cut out pictures of cartoon characters from newspapers and magazines and glue them onto large sheets of paper. They can then draw speech bubbles and write what they think the characters could be saying to each other.

- Students can work in a group or in pairs to create a cartoon about characters they know (e.g., a pet, family) or humorous events they have seen or experienced.

- Cut apart frames from simple cartoons or picture stories for students to sequence correctly.

ADAM'S NEW FRIEND

Name _____

Read the cartoon and answer the questions on the following pages.

ADAM'S NEW FRIEND

Right There   Find the answers directly in the text.

1. What are the children's names? _____

2. How did they get their kites? _____

_____

3. Write the numbers 1 to 6 next to each sentence to show the order of what happened in the cartoon.

  a. _____ The wind became stronger.

  b. _____ A bird was looking at Adam.

  c. _____ They flew their kites at the park.

  d. _____ The children were given kites as a present.

  e. _____ The wind lifted Adam into the air.

  f. _____ Adam landed in a tree.

Think and Search   Think about what the text says.

1. Why didn't Amy take off in the wind?

_____

_____

_____

2. How do you know that the wind was really strong?

_____

_____

ADAM'S NEW FRIEND

Imagine that the bird and Adam talk to each other in the tree. In the speech bubbles, write what you think they would say.

ADAM'S NEW FRIEND

Predicting

Look at the pictures in the cartoon below. In the speech bubbles, write what you think the boy might be saying to himself.

Genre: Mystery

READING FOCUS

- Analyzes and extracts information from a mystery rhyme to answer literal, inferential, and applied questions
- Makes predictions based on the text and background information
- Scans text to locate information

ANSWER KEY

Right There (Page 16)

1. lost

2. thought the bone was under his paw

3. can't find the bone

4. Drawings and answers will vary. Possible answer(s): near the back fence, in the bin, by his kennel, under his paw.

Think and Search (Page 16)

1. Answers will vary.

2. Answers will vary. Possible answer(s): worried, forgetful, determined.

On Your Own (Page 17)

Drawings and answers will vary.

Applying Strategies (Page 18)

1–4. Drawings and answers will vary.

EXTENSIONS

- Students can find pairs of rhyming words in the poem and make lists of other words that also rhyme with them.
- Students can decide "what is lost" and "who lost it," then work with the class to compose a similar text based on the rhyme pattern modeled in "Lost."

For example:

Where did I leave her?
Where can she be?
Do lots of mother cats
Forget like me?

Name _____

Read the mystery rhyme and answer the questions on the following pages.

Where did I hide it?
Where can it be?
Do lots of other puppies
Forget like me?

Is it near the back fence?
Did I hide it in the bin?
I'll have to find it soon,
Or I'll be looking thin.

Where did I hide it?
Where can it be?
Do lots of other puppies
Forget like me?

Did I put it by my kennel?
Wasn't it just right under my paw?
If I don't find it soon,
I'll have to call the law.

Where did I hide it?
Where can it be?
Do lots of other puppies
Forget like me?

I really want to find it.
It's a very special bone.
If you won't help me find it,
I'll do it on my own.

LOST

Place an **X** in the box next to the best answer.

1. The bone is . . .

□ in the bin.   □ by the kennel.   □ lost.   □ under his paw.

2. The puppy . . .

□ thought the bone was under his paw.   □ put the bone near the fence.

□ doesn't want any help.   □ looked under the car.

3. He will call the law if he . . .

□ finds the bone.   □ gets another bone.

□ can't find the bone.   □ wants a drink.

4. Write the names of and draw two places the puppy looked for his bone.

_____   _____

Think and Search   Think about what the text says.

1. Do you think the puppy will find his bone? _____

2. Write some words to describe what the puppy is like.

_____

LOST

On Your Own   Use what you know about the text and your own experience.

Where do you think the puppy hid his bone? Draw and label two more places where he could look.

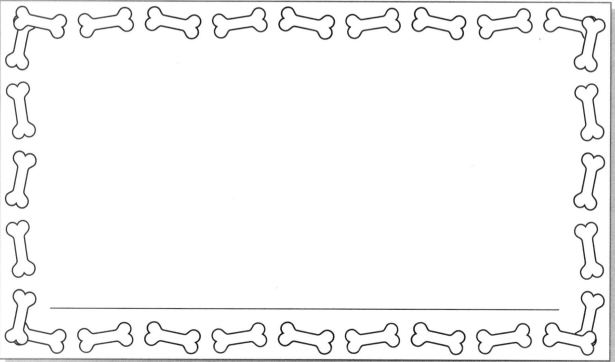

LOST

Making Connections

After reading the text on page 15, make the connection between what you already know and the new information from the text.

1. What is something special you have that you wouldn't like someone to take?

_____

_____

2. Where do you keep it now? _____

3. If you really wanted to hide it so that nobody would find it, where would you put it? Draw your special thing in a really good hiding place.

4. Draw some of the things you have lost and the places where you have found them.

Genre: Play

READING FOCUS

- Analyzes and extracts information from a play to answer literal, inferential, and applied questions
- Makes predictions to determine possible past and future events
- Scans text to locate words with the opposite meaning of those given

---

ANSWER KEY

Right There (Page 21)

1. a. down   b. full   c. open   d. old

2. a. Yes   b. No   c. No   d. No   e. Yes

Think and Search (Page 21)

1. Answers will vary.

2. Answers will vary. Answers should include evidence from the text.

On Your Own (Page 22)

1. Answers will vary.

2. Drawings will vary.

Applying Strategies (Page 23)

1. Drawings and answers will vary.

2. Answers will vary.

EXTENSIONS

- After completing page 23, students can dramatize their stories about how the trunk came to be buried or what happened after it was opened.
- Students can write and continue the dialogue between the characters in the play.

THE TIN TRUNK

Name _____

Read the play and answer the questions on the following pages.

Storyteller:	The children were staying at an old beach cottage. They were digging in the sand around some rocks at the side of the shed.
Tony:	Hey, there is something down here. Come and help me dig it out.
Shannon:	Perhaps it's buried treasure! I'll get my shovel and help you.
Taj:	It looks really old, and it's made out of metal. It's some kind of trunk. Keep digging, Shannon.
Tari:	It could be magic. Perhaps there's a genie in it who can grant us three wishes.
Tony:	What an imagination! You must read tons of books, Tari.
Shannon:	Well, what do you think is in it?
Tony:	Probably some old fishing gear. Let's open it and find out.
Tari:	I'm scared. There might be some magic beans in it, and we can plant them and climb up the beanstalk.
Taj:	Yes, Tari, and find a hen that lays golden eggs, of course. Why don't we just go and ask Mom?
Shannon:	That would be a waste of time. She's reading right now, and she won't even listen to us when she's got her nose in a book.
Tari:	Aunty Sue, Aunty Sue, I'm scared, I'm scared.
Mom:	What's the matter this time, Tari?
Sam:	It's okay, Mom, we've found an old trunk, and she thinks there is something magic in it.
Mom:	I've never seen that before. Why don't you open it up and see?
Shannon:	I hope there is lots of money in it.
Sam:	It's probably full of old photos or toys, but it has a really strange lock on it, which we can't open.
Taj:	I guess we'll just have to wait until Dad gets home from fishing. I wonder what we'll find . . .

THE TIN TRUNK

Right There   Find the answers directly in the text.

1. Find a word in the play that means the opposite of each word.

    a. up _____

    b. empty _____

    c. shut _____

    d. new _____

2. Read each sentence. Choose **Yes** or **No**.

    a. Shannon used a shovel to dig out the trunk.   ❑ Yes   ❑ No

    b. Mom had seen the trunk before.   ❑ Yes   ❑ No

    c. Tari wanted them to open the trunk.   ❑ Yes   ❑ No

    d. Mom told them not to open the trunk.   ❑ Yes   ❑ No

    e. The lock was hard to open.   ❑ Yes   ❑ No

Think and Search   Think about what the text says.

1. Which child do you think is the youngest?

_____

2. What does this child do to make you think this?

_____

_____

_____

_____

THE TIN TRUNK

On Your Own   Use what you know about the text and your own experience.

1. Do you think Dad will be able to open the trunk? _____

2. Draw Dad trying to open the trunk.

THE TIN TRUNK

Use the text on page 20 to complete these activities.

Predicting

1. Draw a picture and write about what you think might be in the trunk.

_____

_____

2. Make up a story about how the trunk was left in the sand, and write the information on the chart.

Who left the trunk?	When was it left there?
Why was it left?	What did the person who left it hope would happen?

Teacher Information

READING FOCUS

- Analyzes and extracts information from a fable to answer literal, inferential, and applied questions
- Makes connections based on prior knowledge and the text
- Compares and makes judgments based on connections made

ANSWER KEY

Right There (Page 26)

1. a. Yes   b. No   c. Yes   d. No   e. Yes

2. a. picture of a shallow dish   b. picture of a long-necked jar

Think and Search (Page 26)

Answers will vary. Possible answer(s):

1. hungry, sad, angry

2. long, tall, thin

3. get even, play a trick, teach him a lesson

4. like, trust, care about

On Your Own (Page 27)

1. Answers will vary.

2. Answers will vary. Possible answer(s): Fox learned that you should treat others the way you would want to be treated.

3. Answers will vary.

4. Fox was not sorry. He was playing a mean trick on Stork.

5. Answers will vary. Possible answer(s): Do not play tricks unless you can take the same treatment yourself; treat others the way you would want to be treated; one bad turn deserves another.

Applying Strategies (Page 28)

1. Drawings will vary.   2–5. Answers will vary.

EXTENSIONS

- The class can read and discuss various fables, particularly the similarities and differences between them; for example, the number of animals featured, their personalities, and the importance and meaning of the morals included.

- The teacher can collect and display books of fables, taking particular note of the different types of illustrations.

- Other Aesop's fables include the following:
  - "The Lion and the Mouse"
  - "The Crow and the Pitcher"
  - "The Ant and the Grasshopper"
  - "The Fox and the Grapes"
  - "The Tortoise and the Hare"
  - "The Frog and the Ox"

Name _____

Read the fable and answer the questions on the following pages.

Fox invited Stork to dinner, and as a joke, he put their soup in shallow dishes. Fox could lap it up, but Stork could only wet the end of his long bill. Poor Stork left, still feeling hungry.

Fox smiled and said, "I'm sorry that you didn't like the soup I made."

"Don't apologize," replied Stork. "Come visit me soon, and I'll make dinner for you."

When Fox went to visit Stork, Stork put their dinner in long-necked jars with narrow mouths. Fox couldn't reach the food, and he just licked the outside of the jar.

"I will not apologize for the dinner," Stork said, "because one bad turn deserves another."

THE STORK AND THE FOX

Right There   Find the answers directly in the text.

1. Read each sentence. Choose **Yes** or **No**.

    a. Fox made some soup for Stork.   ❏ Yes   ❏ No

    b. Stork ate the soup Fox made.   ❏ Yes   ❏ No

    c. Stork invited Fox to come for dinner.   ❏ Yes   ❏ No

    d. Fox enjoyed the dinner that Stork made for him. ❏ Yes   ❏ No

    e. Fox played a trick on Stork.   ❏ Yes   ❏ No

2. Draw the type of dish that was suitable for each character.

a. This is the dish Fox liked.	**b.** This is the dish Stork liked.

Think and Search   Think about what the text says.

Write in the missing words.

    1. Stork was feeling _____ when he left Fox's house.

    2. The jar was too _____ for Fox to reach the soup.

    3. Stork made dinner for Fox because he wanted to _____

    _____.

    4. The two animals did not really _____ each other.

THE STORK AND THE FOX

On Your Own   Use what you know about the text and your own experience.

1. Do you think that Stork was right to play the same trick on Fox that Fox played on him?

_____

_____

2. What do you think Fox learned?

_____

_____

3. Do you think that Fox will play the same trick again? Why or why not?

_____

_____

4. The word *apologize* means to say you are sorry. In the story, Fox said, "I'm sorry that you didn't like the soup I made."

Do you think Fox was really sorry? _____

_____

5. The story of "The Stork and the Fox" is a fable with a moral at the end. What is the moral?

_____

_____

_____

THE STORK AND THE FOX

Making Connections

A saying you may be familiar with is "One good turn deserves another." Think about a time you did something good for someone and in return, they did something positive.

1. Draw a picture of something good you did for another person.

2. For whom did you do something good?

_____

3. What did you do?

_____

_____

_____

4. Did the person do something good for you?

_____

5. How did you feel? _____

_____

Genre: Fantasy

READING FOCUS

- Analyzes and extracts information from a fantasy to answer literal, inferential, and applied questions
- Makes connections between prior knowledge and the information presented in the text

ANSWER KEY

Right There (Page 31)

1. Yes
2. No
3. Yes
4. No
5. Yes

Think and Search (Page 31)

1. a–b. Answers will vary.
2. Answers will vary. Possible answer(s): The little creatures are frustrated with humans.

On Your Own (Page 32)

Drawings and answers will vary.

Applying Strategies (Page 33)

1. Drawings will vary.
2. Answers will vary. Possible answer(s): clear land to build homes, turn the trees into lumber, produce paper.

EXTENSIONS

- Students can create a collage of a forest with different types of trees and the animals that live there.
- Other stories about goblins, elves, and fairies include the following:
  - "The Elves and the Shoemaker"
  - "Cinderella"
  - "Sleeping Beauty"

Name _____

Read the fantasy story and answer the questions on the following pages.

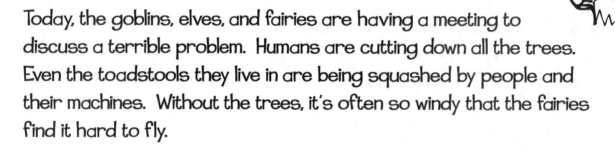

Deep, deep in the forest live the goblins, elves, and fairies. They have lived there for hundreds of years, but very few humans have ever seen them because they run away and hide whenever they hear a noise. They are kind, gentle creatures who work hard and enjoy the peace and quiet of the dark forest.

Today, the goblins, elves, and fairies are having a meeting to discuss a terrible problem. Humans are cutting down all the trees. Even the toadstools they live in are being squashed by people and their machines. Without the trees, it's often so windy that the fairies find it hard to fly.

"I'm sure that they don't want to hurt us," said one of the younger fairies, "but they just don't understand that soon we'll have nowhere to live."

"They don't know about all the things we do to help them," explained an older goblin. "Most of them don't even believe that we exist."

"Some children know about us," one of the elves added, "because they read about us in their storybooks. Let's see if they will help us."

"Yes, that's a great idea! We'll tell them about our problems, and hopefully they will try to stop others from cutting down all the trees. Anyway, I'm sure that they love the forests and will want to try and protect it for their own children to enjoy in the future."

THE LITTLE CREATURES

SAVE OUR TREES!

Right There   Find the answers directly in the text.

Read each sentence. Choose **Yes** or **No**.

1. The little creatures run away when they hear a noise.   ☐ Yes ☐ No

2. Fairies enjoy flying when it's windy.   ☐ Yes ☐ No

3. The little creatures held a meeting.   ☐ Yes ☐ No

4. Most people believe that fairies, elves, and goblins exist.   ☐ Yes ☐ No

5. The little creatures are going to ask the children to help them save the trees.   ☐ Yes ☐ No

Think and Search   Think about what the text says.

1. **a.** Do you think the children will want to help the little creatures? _____

b. Give two reasons.

_____

_____

_____

2. How do you think the little creatures feel about humans?

_____

_____

_____

THE LITTLE CREATURES

On Your Own   Use what you know about the text and your own experience.

Draw and write about how you and your friends could help the little creatures.

_____

_____

_____

THE LITTLE CREATURES

After reading the text on page 30, make the connection between what you already know and the new information from the text.

1. Create a poster encouraging people not to cut down too many trees. Make your poster bright and colorful.

2. List some reasons people cut down trees.

- _____

- _____

- _____

- _____

Genre: Procedure

Teacher Information

READING FOCUS

- Analyzes and extracts information from a procedure to answer literal, inferential, and applied questions
- Makes connections between text and personal experience

ANSWER KEY

Right There (Page 36)

1. a. Yes   b. No   c. No   d. Yes

2. a. 4   b. 1   c. 6   d. 2   e. 5   f. 3

Think and Search (Page 36)

1. strawberry – red, kiwifruit – green, banana – yellow, grape – green, watermelon – red

2. To continue the color pattern without having the same color placed consecutively

On Your Own (Page 37)

1. Safer for kids to cut fruit with

2. To prevent kids from accidently poking and hurting themselves

3. a. Answers will vary.

   b. Drawings will vary.

Applying Strategies (Page 38)

1. Answers will vary.

2. Drawings will vary.

EXTENSIONS

- Students may enjoy reading and following simple recipes in children's cookbooks. Here are some suitable titles:
  - *The Healthy Body Cookbook: Over 50 Fun Activities and Delicious Recipes for Kids* by Joan D'Amico and Karen Eich Drummond
  - *Better Homes and Gardens New Junior Cookbook* by Jennifer Dorland Darling
  - *Pretend Soup and Other Recipes* by Moelie Katzen and Anne Henderson
  - *A First Cookbook for Children* by Evelyne Johnson
  - *Betty Crocker's Kids Cook* by Betty Crocker

Name _____

Read the procedure and answer the questions on the following pages.

You will need:

- strawberries, kiwifruit, banana, green grapes, watermelon

- container of strawberry yogurt

- cutting board

- blunt knife

- paper towels

- small bowl

- teaspoon

- wooden skewers with the sharp ends removed

Directions:

1. Wash the fruit and pat dry with the paper towels.

2. Peel and cut the kiwifruit, banana, and watermelon into chunks.

3. Carefully thread one piece of each fruit onto a skewer.

4. Continue until all the fruit is used.

5. Put some yogurt into a small bowl.

6. Spread a teaspoon of yogurt onto a fruit skewer and eat!

FRUITY SNACKS

Right There   Find the answers directly in the text.

1. Read each sentence. Choose **Yes** or **No**.

   a. The fruit is washed.   ☐ Yes ☐ No

   b. The grapes are cut into chunks.   ☐ Yes ☐ No

   c. Metal skewers are used.   ☐ Yes ☐ No

   d. The grapes are green.   ☐ Yes ☐ No

2. Write the numbers 1 to 6 next to each sentence to show the order of how to make the fruity snacks.

   a. _____ Continue until all the fruit is used.

   b. _____ Wash the fruit and pat dry with the paper towels.

   c. _____ Spread a teaspoon of yogurt onto a fruit skewer and eat!

   d. _____ Peel and cut the kiwifruit, banana, and watermelon into chunks.

   e. _____ Put some yogurt into a small bowl.

   f. _____ Carefully thread one piece of each fruit onto a skewer.

Think and Search   Think about what the text says.

1. Color the fruit on the skewer correctly.

2. Why were green grapes used and not red?

   _____

   _____

FRUITY SNACKS

On Your Own   Use what you know about the text and your own experience.

1. Why is a blunt knife used?

    _____

    _____

2. Why are the sharp ends removed from the skewers?

    _____

    _____

3. a. What is another way to prepare a healthy snack, using some or all of
        the ingredients from the original recipe? What other ingredients would
        you add?

    _____

    _____

    _____

    b. Draw a picture of your new healthy snack.

FRUITY SNACKS

After reading the text on page 35, make the connection between what you already know and the new information.

1. Would you change any of the ingredients if you wanted to make the fruity snacks? Place an **X** next to the fruits and the toppings you would like to choose from. Include any other fruits or toppings you wish to add.

Fruits	**Toppings**
❑ strawberries	❑ strawberry yogurt
❑ grapes	❑ banana yogurt
❑ bananas	❑ vanilla yogurt
❑ kiwifruit	❑ whipped cream
❑ watermelon	❑ chocolate topping
❑ peaches	❑ _____
❑ pineapple	❑ _____
❑ _____	
❑ _____	

2. Draw a picture of your fruity snack on the skewer below.

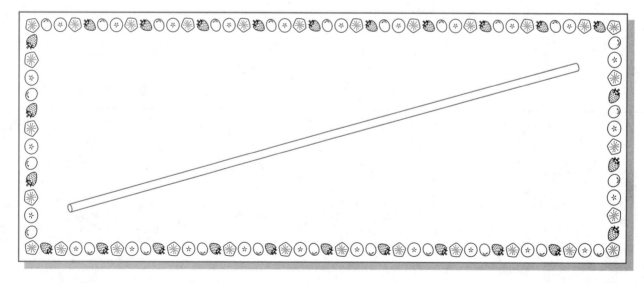

Genre: Timetable

READING FOCUS

- Analyzes and extracts information from a timetable to answer literal, inferential, and applied questions
- Compares information from text with own written information
- Scans text to locate information

ANSWER KEY

Right There (Page 41)

1. a. music practice

   b. she brushes her teeth

2. a. No   b. Yes   c. Yes   d. No   e. Yes

Think and Search (Page 41)

1. Answers will vary. Possible answer(s): Sarah doesn't need to practice music on Tuesday.

2. Answers will vary.

On Your Own (Page 42)

1. Drawings and answers will vary.

Applying Strategies (Page 43)

1. Answers will vary.

2. a–d. Answers will vary.

3. a–c. Answers will vary.

EXTENSIONS

- Students can formulate questions to ask each other about both Sarah's and their own individual timetables.
- Collect different types of timetables (bus schedule, TV listings, movie times, etc.) for students to practice reading. Model how to read various formats of timetables.

SARAH'S TIMETABLE

Name _____

Read the timetable and answer the questions on the following pages.

TIME (PM)	MONDAY	TUESDAY
3:30	home from school	home from school
	afternoon snack	afternoon snack
4:00	play with friends	get ready for music
		drive to music
4:30	play with friends	music lesson
5:00	watch TV	drive home
		shop with Mom
5:30	watch TV	watch TV
6:00	dinner	dinner
6:30	music practice	watch TV
7:00	shower and pajamas	shower and pajamas
7:30	reading or homework	reading or homework
8:00	brush teeth	brush teeth
	story in bed and sleep	story in bed and sleep

SARAH'S TIMETABLE

Right There Find the answers directly in the text.

1. Complete each sentence with information from the timetable.

    a. On Monday, at 6:30, Sarah has _____.

    b. Sarah reads or does homework right before _____

    _____.

2. Read each sentence. Choose **Yes** or **No**.

    a. Sarah watches more TV on Monday. ☐ Yes ☐ No

    b. Dinner is at the same time on both days. ☐ Yes ☐ No

    c. Sarah puts on her pajamas before she brushes her teeth. ☐ Yes ☐ No

    d. Sarah watches TV before her music lesson. ☐ Yes ☐ No

    e. Sarah and her friends play before her music practice. ☐ Yes ☐ No

Think and Search Think about what the text says.

1. Why do you think Sarah is allowed to watch TV after dinner on Tuesday?

_____

_____

2. Which day do you think is busier? Why?

_____

_____

SARAH'S TIMETABLE

On Your Own   Use what you know about the text and your own experience.

Draw a picture to show the time in Sarah's day that you think is the best. Give a reason at the bottom for why you chose that time.

_____

_____

_____

SARAH'S TIMETABLE

After completing your timetable, make a comparison by thinking more specifically about the similarities and differences between your day and Sarah's.

1. Complete this timetable for one day to show what you do after school.

Time (PM)	Day of the Week: _____
3:30	
4:00	
4:30	
5:00	
5:30	
6:00	
6:30	
7:00	
7:30	
8:00	

2. Read your timetable, and answer the following questions.

   a. What time did you have dinner?

   _____

   b. Did you play with your friends?

   _____

   c. Did you watch TV after dinner?

   _____

   d. Did you go to bed after 8 o'clock?

   _____

3. Look at one day of Sarah's timetable on page 40 and compare it with yours.

   a. Who had dinner earlier?

   _____

   b. Who spent more time watching TV?

   _____

   c. Which timetable do you like better? Why?

   _____

   _____

   _____

   _____

Genre: Letter

READING FOCUS

- Analyzes and extracts information from a letter to answer literal, inferential, and applied questions
- Compares information in a text to his/her own experiences
- Makes connections between events in a text and his/her own experience

ANSWER KEY

Right There (Page 46)

1. a. Caris   b. Aunty Kerry
2. breakfast sandwiches and hot chocolate
3. The letter is about a camping trip.
4. Mom gave Ryan a coloring book to stop him from whining.

Think and Search (Page 46)

1. hike, play with friends, or play on the adventure playground
2. a. Yes   b. No   c. Yes   d. Yes

On Your Own (Page 47)

Drawings and answers will vary.

Applying Strategies (Page 48)

Answers will vary.

EXTENSIONS

- Students may enjoy reading the following series of books:
  - *The Jolly Postman (or Other People's Letters)* by Janet and Allan Ahlberg
  - *The Jolly Pocket Postman* by Janet and Allan Ahlberg
  - *The Jolly Christmas Postman* by Janet and Allan Ahlberg

Name _____

Read the letter and answer the questions on the following pages.

Dear Aunty Kerry,

I am writing to tell you about the camping trip we went on over summer vacation. Mom and Dad woke Ryan and me up at 5 o'clock in the morning. It was still dark! We ate our breakfast in the car while Dad drove. Mom had made breakfast sandwiches and a thermos of hot chocolate.

It took three hours to drive to the campsite. I listened to music on my music player. Ryan whined a lot because he was bored. Mom gave him a coloring book, which kept him quiet for a while.

When we got there, we helped unpack the car and set up the tent. Then, we went exploring with Mom and Dad. Several other families were also staying there. One family had a girl my age and a boy Ryan's age. We played together a lot.

There was so much to do at the camp. We could swim, go canoeing, or fish in the lake. Dad and Ryan caught a huge trout. They were very pleased! We also went hiking, except Ryan had to be carried some of the way. At the campsite there was an adventure playground with a fort and a wobbly bridge.

We had a great time, and I was sad to leave. Hope to see you soon.

Love,
   Caris

THE CAMPING TRIP

| **Right There** | Find the answers directly in the text. |

1. Answer the following questions.

    a. Who wrote the letter? _____

    b. To whom was the letter written? _____

2. What did the children have for breakfast in the car?

_____

3. Place an **X** in the box next to the best answer.

    ❏ The letter is about the school holidays.

    ❏ The letter is about a camping trip.

    ❏ The letter is about catching a fish.

4. How did Mom stop Ryan from whining in the car?

_____

| **Think and Search** | Think about what the text says. |

1. List two more things the children could do on the camping trip.

    swim, go canoeing, fish, _____ , _____

2. Read each sentence. Choose **Yes** or **No**.

    a. The children made friends at the camp.   ❏ Yes   ❏ No

    b. Ryan is older than Caris.   ❏ Yes   ❏ No

    c. Ryan got tired on the hike.   ❏ Yes   ❏ No

    d. The children would have liked to stay longer.   ❏ Yes   ❏ No

THE CAMPING TRIP

Use what you know about the text and your own experience.

Draw and write about what you would like to have done if you were at the campsite.

_____

_____

_____

_____

THE CAMPING TRIP

Making Connections

Read about Caris's camping trip below. Then think about a time you went on a camping trip or another kind of vacation, or imagine you have been on one. Complete the empty boxes with words or pictures about your trip.

	Caris	You
a. Where did she/you go?	a camping trip	
b. How did she/you get there?	by car	
c. When did she/you leave?	5:00 a.m.	
d. How long did it take to get there?	three hours	
e. What did she/you do on the way?	• ate breakfast • listened to music	
f. Where did she/you stay?	in a tent at a campsite	
g. What did she/you do there?	• fished • went canoeing • swam • played with new friends • played on the adventure playground • went hiking	

48

READING FOCUS

- Analyzes and extracts information from a folktale to answer literal, inferential, and applied questions
- Makes comparisons between the past and the present by using personal background knowledge and some information from the text
- Creates visual images based on sensory imaging

ANSWER KEY

Right There (Page 51)

1. Yes 2. No 3. Yes 4. Yes 5. No

Think and Search (Page 51)

1. Answers will vary. Possible answer(s): Johnny Appleseed was generous, kind, helpful, friendly, and kind to animals.

2. Answers will vary. Possible answer(s): They respected him because he gave them apple seeds to plant.

3. Answers will vary. Possible answer(s): He was a hard-working man who spent a good part of his life outside, planting and working with his hands.

On Your Own (Page 52)

1. Answers will vary.   2. Drawing of tree with all five parts clearly labeled

Applying Strategies (Page 53)

1. Answers will vary. Possible answer(s):
   See: sky, trees, animals, people
   Hear: birds, water flowing in a river, leaves rustling
   Smell: grass, plants, wild flowers
   Touch: dirt, grass

2. Answers will vary. Possible answer(s):
   Then food—hunt for wild game, grow their own crops
   clothing—used to protect from elements more than fashion; neutral colors
   transportation—by foot, horseback, horse-drawn wagon, natural water ways, trains
   housing—simple four-wall structure

   Now food—purchase food in a grocery story, eat out at restaurants
   clothing—fashionable, colorful
   transportation—plains, trains, cars
   housing—apartments, condominiums, houses

EXTENSIONS

- Read and discuss other folktales about past heroes and where and when they lived. For example, Ned Kelly in Australia, Joan of Arc in France, and King Arthur in Britain.

- The class can play the telephone game to demonstrate to students how a simple story can be changed, unintentionally, by many retellings.

JOHNNY APPLESEED

Name _____

Read the folktale and answer the questions on the following pages.

Johnny Chapman traveled around America over 200 years ago with a bag of apple seeds on his back. He sold small apple trees he had grown and gave seeds away to the settlers and the Native Americans. He gained the nickname Johnny Appleseed after years of selling apple trees.

He was a kind, gentle man who wanted to plant apple trees so that no one would ever be hungry. With his cooking pot worn on his head like a hat, and without any shoes, he traveled alone, making friends with everyone. He was especially popular with the children and even became friends with some of the wild animals he came across.

Many interesting stories are told about him, but they may not all be true. One such story is about a bear and its cubs sleeping inside a hollow tree trunk with Johnny one night during a snowstorm. They did not attack him, and he left safely the next day.

Another story is about a rattlesnake that tried to bite him but couldn't get its fangs through his skin because it was "as tough as an elephant's hide."

Stories like these that people tell each other are called "tall tales."

It is amazing that some of the trees Johnny Appleseed planted so long ago are still growing. Even today, people are eating and enjoying apples from these trees.

JOHNNY APPLESEED

Right There   Find the answers directly in the text.

Read each sentence. Choose **Yes** or **No**.

1. Children liked Johnny Appleseed.   ❏ Yes   ❏ No

2. Johnny Appleseed wore shoes all the time.   ❏ Yes   ❏ No

3. He made friends with some wild animals.   ❏ Yes   ❏ No

4. The pot he wore on his head was for cooking.   ❏ Yes   ❏ No

5. All of the trees he planted have died.   ❏ Yes   ❏ No

Think and Search   Think about what the text says.

1. Write three reasons why you think people liked Johnny Appleseed.

    • _____

    • _____

    • _____

2. How did Native Americans most likely feel about Johnny Appleseed?

    _____

    _____

3. Why might Johnny Appleseed's skin be "as tough as an elephant's hide"?

    _____

    _____

JOHNNY APPLESEED

On Your Own   Use what you know about the text and your own experience.

1. Which of the two tall tales about Johnny Appleseed do you think is more likely to be true? Give a reason for why you think this.

    _____

    _____

    _____

    _____

2. Draw an apple tree, and label the tree with these parts:

    branches   leaves   fruit   roots   trunk

JOHNNY APPLESEED

Sensory Imaging

After reading the text on page 50, complete the following activity by using your senses to create a mental image of what you have read.

1. Imagine you are Johnny Appleseed walking through the woods. Write down what you might see, hear, smell, and touch.

See: _____

Hear: _____

Smell: _____

Touch: _____

Comparing

Make a comparison by thinking more specifically about the similarities and differences.

2. Johnny Appleseed lived over 200 years ago. Think about the similarities and differences between then and now to complete the chart.

Then	Now
food	food
clothing	clothing
transportation	transportation
housing	housing

Genre: Science Fiction

READING FOCUS

- Analyzes and extracts information from a science-fiction narrative to answer literal, inferential, and applied questions
- Uses sensory imaging to complete an illustration
- Makes predictions based on text, personal background, and experience

ANSWER KEY

Right There (Page 56)

1. a. Planet Zog

    b. by spaceship

    c. Earthlings

2. a. gasped   b. politely   c. strange

3. a. False   b. False   c. True   d. True

Think and Search (Page 56)

1. The spaceship landing and taking off.

2. Answers will vary.

On Your Own (Page 57)

1. The aliens have never seen humans before.

2. Drawings will vary.

Applying Strategies (Page 58)

1. Drawings will vary.

2. Answers will vary.

EXTENSIONS

- Books containing science fiction suitable for this age group include the following:
    - *There's No Place Like Space: All About Our Solar System* (Cat in the Hat's Learning Library) by Tish Rabe
    - *Aliens for Breakfast* by Stephanie Spinner and Jonathon Etra
    - *Commander Toad in Space* by Jane Yolen

Name _____

Read the science-fiction story and answer the questions on the following pages.

"Jake! Do you want to come to the park and play soccer?" yelled my older brother, Harry.

"Sure do!" I yelled back.

We raced over to the park and began to kick the ball. Harry kicked it so hard it went into the bushes. He came to help me find it.

Suddenly, we heard a strange whirring noise and a *swoosh*! Ducking down behind the bushes, we peered out. We gasped in surprise. A spaceship had just landed! It had "Planet Zog" written on the side.

A little door opened, and out hopped two aliens. They looked around and then hopped up to a tree. "Hello, Earthling," said the aliens politely. The tree didn't say a word. They hopped up to a trash can. "Hello, Earthling," they said again. The trash can didn't say a word. Next, they hopped up to a faucet. "Hello, Earthling," they said once more. The faucet didn't say a word.

The aliens looked at each other. "The Earthlings have not learned how to speak yet," one of them said. "Let's come back another time."

So, with a *whirr* and a *swoosh*, they zoomed off into space.

A VISIT FROM PLANET ZOG

Right There   Find the answers directly in the text.

1. Answer the following questions.

    a. Where did the aliens come from? _____

    b. How did they arrive on Earth? _____

    c. What did they call the people on Earth? _____

2. Match each word in the story to its meaning.

    a. took a sudden, quick breath of air   • politely

    b. speaking with good manners   • gasped

    c. unusual or odd   • strange

3. Read each sentence. Decide if each statement is **True** or **False**.

    a. Jake kicked the ball into the bushes.   ☐ True   ☐ False

    b. There were three aliens.   ☐ True   ☐ False

    c. The aliens moved by hopping.   ☐ True   ☐ False

    d. The boys were playing soccer.   ☐ True   ☐ False

Think and Search   Think about what the text says.

1. What made the strange whirring and swooshing noises?

_____

2. Do you think the aliens were friendly? Explain your answer.

_____

_____

A VISIT FROM PLANET ZOG

On Your Own   Use what you know about the text and your own experience.

1. Why do you think the aliens thought the tree, trash can, and faucet were people?

_____

_____

2. Draw something else in the park the aliens might have thought was an Earthling.

A VISIT FROM PLANET ZOG

Sensory Imaging

After reading the text on page 55, complete the following activity by using your senses to create a mental image of what you have read.

1. The picture of the aliens on page 55 does not show their faces. Close your eyes, and imagine what their faces might look like. Draw their faces in the outlines below and color them in.

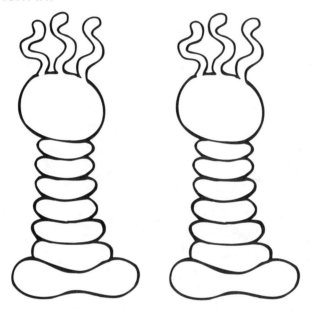

2. Imagine you are Jake. You and Harry have decided to come out from behind the bushes to talk to the aliens. Write what you think you and the aliens would say to each other in the speech bubbles.

Predicting

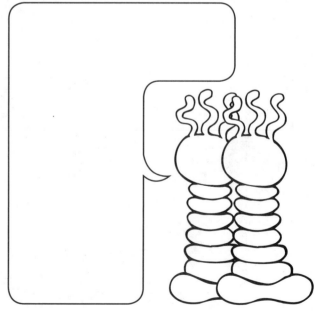

Genre: Map

READING FOCUS

- Analyzes and extracts information from a map to answer literal, inferential, and applied questions
- Uses sensory imaging to appreciate the locations shown on the map
- Makes connections between points on the map

ANSWER KEY

Right There (Page 61)

1. Holiday Island Tourist Resort in cabins

2. horseback riding, canoeing, tennis, play at the playground, ride bikes, swimming, picnic, shopping

3. a. False   b. True   c. False   d. True

Think and Search (Page 61)

1. There are plenty of outdoor activities.

2. Answers will vary. Possible answer(s): along the coast, grass area, hills.

3. Answers will vary. Possible answer(s): horse caretaker, clerk at supermarket, waiter/chef at the restaurant, lifeguard at the pool, worker at the bike shop, cleaner of the cabins, landscaper, worker at the chapel.

On Your Own (Page 62)

1. Drawings will vary.   2. Answers will vary.   3. Answers will vary.

Applying Strategies (Page 63)

1. a. Answers will vary. Possible answer(s): hike, canoe, play tennis, swim, go to the beach, horseback ride, play at the playground, picnic, barbecue, shop, eat at the restaurant.

   b. Answers will vary. Possible answer(s): waves crashing in the shoreline, birds chirping, children playing, water splashing in the pool, meat sizzling on the grill, leaves rustling.

   c. Answers will vary. Possible answer(s): sunblock lotion; salty, ocean air; barbecue.

   d. Answers will vary. Possible answer(s): food from the supermarket, barbecue.

   e. Answers will vary. Possible answer(s): sand, saltwater, grass, horse, trees.

   f–g. Answers will vary.

2. Answers will vary.

EXTENSIONS

- Students can study other simple maps and draw their own Holiday Island map.
- Students can read literature involving maps or create story maps from stories.

HOLIDAY ISLAND

Name _____

Study the map and answer the questions on the following pages.

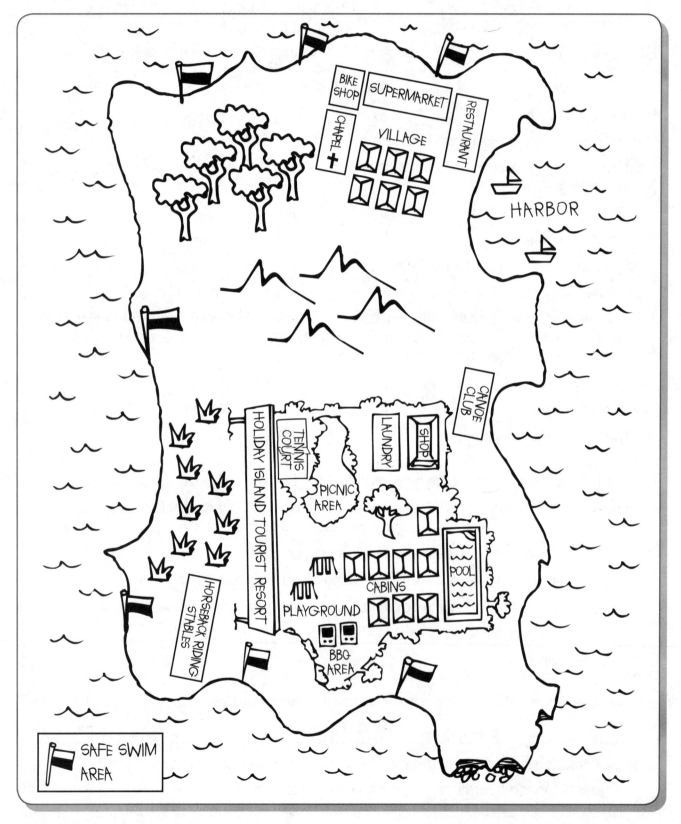

HOLIDAY ISLAND

Right There   Find the answers directly in the text.

1. Where do tourists stay on Holiday Island?

_____

2. List the activities you can do on Holiday Isand.

_____

_____

3. Read each sentence. Decide if each statement is **True** or **False**.

    a. The trees are next to the rocky cliffs .   ☐ True ☐ False

    b. The village is close to the harbor .   ☐ True ☐ False

    c. The hills are near the sea.   ☐ True ☐ False

    d. There are many safe beaches for swimming .   ☐ True ☐ False

Think and Search   Think about what the text says.

1. Why is Holiday Island a great place to visit if you enjoy doing things outside?

_____

_____

2. Name some places you could go through on a horseback ride.

_____

3. List four jobs people who live in the village might have.

    • _____   • _____

    • _____   • _____

HOLIDAY ISLAND

On Your Own   Use what you know about the text and your own experience.

1. Draw pictures of yourself doing two enjoyable activities on the island. Label each picture.

2. Why do you like these activities?

_____

_____

_____

3. Where would you like to spend your next vacation?

_____

_____

HOLIDAY ISLAND

Sensory Imaging

Using the map on page 60, complete the following activity by using your senses to create a mental image of a day spent on Holiday Island.

1. It is your first day on Holiday Island. Explore and write about it below.

    a. What can I do?

    _____

    b. What can I hear?

    _____

    c. What can I smell?

    _____

    d. What can I taste?

    _____

    e. What can I touch?

    _____

    f. How I feel:

    _____

    g. Who I went with:

    _____

2. How much did you enjoy your vacation? Color the beach balls to rate it.

Urk! ⟶ Grrreat!

READING FOCUS

- Analyzes and extracts information from a humorous story to answer literal, inferential, and applied questions

- Uses sensory imaging to answer questions about the humorous story

- Summarizes information to retell the story within a given framework

- Scans text to seek specific information to provide answers

ANSWER KEY

Right There (Page 66)

1. The baby monkey was holding a banana.

2. The baby monkey tickled Timothy under the arms.

3. A bright flash from a camera upset the monkeys.

Think and Search (Page 66)

1. a. False   b. True   c. False   d. True

2. It's not every day you see a boy up in a tree with a monkey.

On Your Own (Page 67)

1. Answers will vary.

2. Answers will vary.

3. Timothy   Mrs. James   zookeeper

Applying Strategies (Page 68)

1. Answers will vary.

2. Answers will vary.

EXTENSIONS

- Students can continue the story from page 65.
- Students can research the countries of origin of zoo animals.
- Students can make a collection of humorous stories involving animals.

Name _____

Read the humorous story and answer the questions on the following pages.

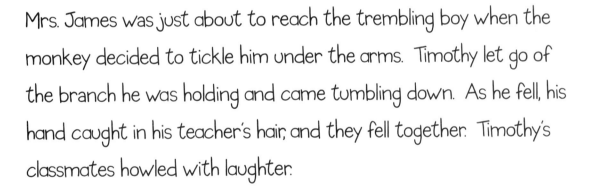

"For the last time, calm down!" screeched Mrs. James to her class as she tried to help Timothy down from the tree in the monkey enclosure.

"How on Earth did you get yourself into this mess?" she grumbled at the frightened boy as a baby monkey fed him a banana.

Mrs. James was just about to reach the trembling boy when the monkey decided to tickle him under the arms. Timothy let go of the branch he was holding and came tumbling down. As he fell, his hand caught in his teacher's hair, and they fell together. Timothy's classmates howled with laughter.

By now, a zookeeper had arrived to rescue the teacher and her student. A sudden bright flash from a camera upset two monkeys, and they jumped onto the zookeeper before she could shut the gate. In an instant, three mischieveous monkeys hopped down from their branches and dashed down the path toward the children's playground.

MONKEY BUSINESS AT THE ZOO

Right There Find the answers directly in the text.

1. Place an **X** in the box next to the correct statement.

   ❑ The baby monkey was wearing a hat.

   ❑ The baby monkey was waving a flag.

   ❑ The baby monkey was holding a banana.

2. What happened to make Timothy let go of the branch?

   _____

   _____

3. What made the monkeys jump onto the zookeeper?

   _____

   _____

Think and Search Think about what the text says.

1. Read each sentence. Decide if each statement is **True** or **False**.

   a. Timothy's classmates were miserable. ❑ True ❑ False

   b. The monkeys were having a good day. ❑ True ❑ False

   c. Timothy was an obedient boy. ❑ True ❑ False

   d. Timothy was ticklish. ❑ True ❑ False

2. Why do you think people were taking pictures?

   _____

   _____

MONKEY BUSINESS AT THE ZOO

On Your Own   Use what you know about the text and your own experience.

1. Imagine you are one of the characters from the story. Draw and write about the character below.

Character: _____   What did your character …

feel? _____

see? _____

taste? _____

smell? _____

hear? _____

2. What do you think the zookeeper might have said to Mrs. James when the panic was all over? Write what you think she might have said in the speech bubble.

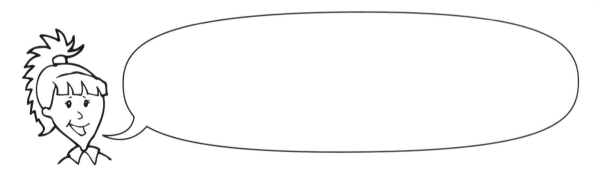

3. Draw a face to show how each person felt about the day.

Timothy   Mrs. James   zookeeper

Name _____

MONKEY BUSINESS AT THE ZOO

Predicting

How strange it would have been to see three monkeys running down the path! What mischief do you think they may have made before being caught?

1. Use the boxes below to help write ideas and plan a story about the monkeys' adventure.

Title: _____

Running down the path.	At the playground.
Who joined in?	Who caught them? How were they captured?
How did the adventure end?	

2. Use this story map to write a fun adventure story. Share it with a friend or the class.

Genre: Poster

READING FOCUS

- Analyzes and extracts information from a poster to answer literal, inferential, and applied questions
- Uses sensory imaging to determine the atmosphere of a performance

---

ANSWER KEY

Right There (Page 71)

1. O'Leary's Magnificent Leprechaun Show
2. two performances
3. a park

Think and Search (Page 71)

1. The poster mentions bringing blankets.
2. Answers will vary. Possible answer(s): dance, sing along, find the pot of gold.
3. Answers will vary.

On Your Own (Page 72)

Answers will vary. Possible answer(s):

Good Things—plenty of space, fresh air, can have a picnic, kids can run around

Bad Things—risk of bad weather, may not have enough shade on a hot day, may be hard to see the performance without a stage

Applying Strategies (Page 73)

1. Answers will vary.
2. a. Answers will vary. Possible answer(s): music, laughter, birds.
   b. Answers will vary. Possible answer(s): people dancing, singing, laughing, having a picnic, leprechauns performing.
   c. Answers will vary. Possible answer(s): food from the picnic baskets.
3. Drawings/answers will vary.
4. Answers will vary.
5. Drawings will vary.

EXTENSIONS

- Students can collect posters or fliers for local activities.
- Students can design posters for current school activities.
- Students can use a poster as a prompt to present a mini-topic on a chosen subject.

Name _____

Read the poster and answer the questions on the following pages.

O'Leary's Magnificent Leprechaun Show

Come and enjoy O'Leary's Magnificent Leprechaun Show!

- ✿ singing
- ✿ music
- ✿ dancing
- ✿ magic tricks
- ✿ daring gymnastic feats

The world's one and only performing leprechaun company

Performances at Coolin Park at 3 p.m. and 7 p.m.
Friday, May 22, through Sunday, May 24
Bring your picnic baskets and blankets.

Join in the fun for your chance to find the pot of gold at the end of the rainbow!

Tickets

adult	$10
family	$25 (2 adults & 2 children)
child	$5 (under 16 years)
	under 4 years free

Available from:
Tourist Office
57 Main Street
South Bend, Indiana 46617

O'LEARY'S LEPRECHAUN SHOW

Right There   Find the answers directly in the text.

1. What is the name of the show?

_____

2. How many performances will there be each day? _____

3. Place an **X** in the box next to the correct answer.

The shows are taking place in . . .

☐ a theater.

☐ a stadium.

☐ a park.

Think and Search   Think about what the text says.

1. What clue is there on the poster to suggest that there is no seating provided at the shows?

_____

_____

2. What things might you do to join in with the fun of the show?

_____

_____

3. How much would it cost your family to attend the show?

_____

_____

O'LEARY'S LEPRECHAUN SHOW

On Your Own   Use what you know about the text and your own experience.

What do you think would be the good things and bad things about having a performance in a park?

Write your ideas for both in the boxes.

Good Things

_____

_____

_____

_____

_____

_____

_____

Bad Things

_____

_____

_____

_____

_____

_____

_____

Name _____

O'LEARY'S LEPRECHAUN SHOW

Sensory Imaging

What fun! A leprechaun show is coming to town! Complete the following activity by using your senses to create a mental image.

1. Who will go with you to the show?

_____

_____

2. What do you think you will . . .

a. hear? _____

_____

b. see? _____

_____

c. taste? _____

_____

3. Draw or write what you will put into your picnic basket.

4. Do you think someone will find the pot of gold?

☐ Yes   ☐ No

Explain your answer.

_____

_____

_____

_____

5. Draw the leprechaun in his costume.

READING FOCUS

- Analyzes and extracts information from a limerick to answer literal, inferential, and applied questions
- Makes connections to choose appropriate rhyming words within the context of a limerick
- Determines important information to illustrate what happened in a limerick

---

ANSWER KEY

Right There (Page 76)

1. a. Bree

   b. She only liked to watch TV.

   c. Her eyes became square.

   d. She got stuck to the chair.

2. square, chair   3. Bree, TV, free   4. five

Think and Search (Page 76)

1. a. Answers will vary. Possible answer(s): Her eyes were ruined from watching too much TV.

   b. Answers will vary. Possible answer(s): She never took a break from watching TV and never got out of her chair.

2. No. The poem ended with Bree not being free.

On Your Own (Page 77)

1. Answers will vary.

2. Drawings/labels will vary.

Applying Strategies (Page 78)

1. Bree, TV, free   2. square, chair   3. Answers will vary.   4. Drawings will vary.

EXTENSIONS

- Books containing limericks and other nonsense poems suitable for this age group include the following:
  - *The Mammoth Book of Jokes* by Geoff Tibballs
  - *The Usborne Book of Jokes* by Philip Hawthorn
  - *Rhymes, Riddles, and Nonsense* by Dr. Seuss
  - *There's an Awful Lot of Weirdos in Our Neighbourhood: A Book of Rather Silly Poems and Pictures* by Colin McNaughton

Name _____

Read the limerick and answer the questions on the following pages.

> There once was a girl named Bree,
>
> Who would only watch the TV.
>
> Her eyes became square,
>
> And she stuck to the chair.
>
> Never again was she free!

A GIRL NAMED BREE

Right There   Find the answers directly in the text.

1. Answer the questions.

  a. What was the girl's name? _____

  b. What did she like to do? _____

  c. What happened to her eyes? _____

  d. What did she get stuck to? _____

2. Copy two words from the limerick that rhyme with *bear*.

  a. _____   **b.** _____

3. Copy three words from the limerick that rhyme with *sea*.

  a. _____   **b.** _____

  c. _____

4. How many lines are in the limerick? _____

Think and Search   Think about what the text says.

1. Why do you think …

  a. Bree's eyes became square? _____

  _____

  b. she stuck to the chair? _____

  _____

  _____

2. Did the limerick have a happy ending?   ☐ Yes   ☐ No

  Why? _____

  _____

A GIRL NAMED BREE

On Your Own   Use what you know about the text and your own experience.

1. What is your favorite TV show?

   _____

   _____

2. Draw and label a picture about it.

A GIRL NAMED BREE

Determining Importance

A limerick is a nonsense poem made up of five lines. Limericks follow a special pattern.

1. Underline in red the words that rhyme in lines 1, 2, and 5.

2. Underline in blue the words that rhyme in lines 3 and 4. These lines have fewer syllables than the others.

There once was a girl named Bree,

Who would only watch the TV.

Her eyes became square,

And she stuck to the chair.

Never again was she free!

3. Complete the limerick below. Follow the rhyming pattern.

There once was a clown from France,

Who wanted to learn how to _____.

He tripped over his toes,

And fell on his _____,

And got mud all over his _____ !

4. Draw a picture of what happened to the clown.

Genre: Book Cover

READING FOCUS

- Analyzes and extracts information from a book cover to answer literal, inferential, and applied questions
- Scans for relevant information
- Makes connections between a book cover viewed and one he/she creates
- Makes predictions based on a visual text

ANSWER KEY

Right There (Page 81)

1. a. *Captain Fishhook and the Buried Treasure*

   b. Ben Black

   c. Molly Morgan

2. the adventures of Captain Fishhook

3. the *Jolly Rascal*

Think and Search (Page 81)

1. The author writes the book.

2. The illustrator draws the illustrations (pictures) for the book.

On Your Own (Page 82)

1. a. Answers will vary.   b. Answers will vary.

2. Drawings will vary.

Applying Strategies (Page 83)

1. Answers will vary. Check book cover for accuracy.

2. Answers will vary.

EXTENSIONS

- Students can view and discuss a variety of book covers, including fiction and nonfiction books, as well as comics, newspapers, and magazines.
- Students can share their favorite books with the class and discuss whether the book cover played a part in their choices.

Name _____

Read the book cover and answer the questions on the following pages.

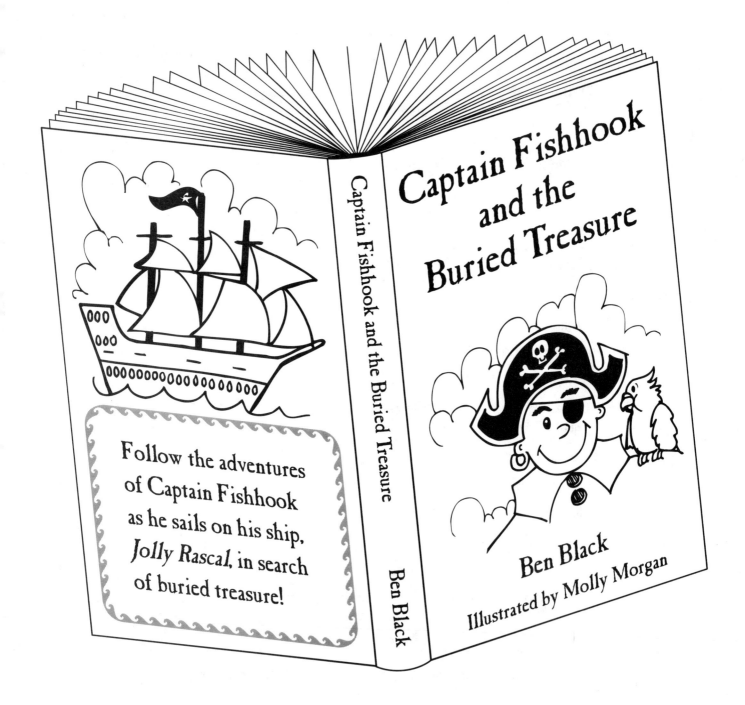

Follow the adventures of Captain Fishhook as he sails on his ship, *Jolly Rascal*, in search of buried treasure!

Captain Fishhook and the Buried Treasure

Ben Black

Captain Fishhook and the Buried Treasure

Ben Black

Illustrated by Molly Morgan

CAPTAIN FISHHOOK AND THE BURIED TREASURE

Right There   Find the answers directly in the text.

1. Answer the questions.

   a. What is the title of the book? _____

   _____

   b. Who is the author? _____

   c. Who is the illustrator? _____

2. Complete the sentence using some words from the book cover.

   The book is about _____

   _____.

3. What is the name of the ship? _____

Think and Search   Think about what the text says.

1. What does the author of a book do? _____

   _____

2. What does the illustrator of a book do? _____

   _____

CAPTAIN FISHHOOK AND THE BURIED TREASURE

On Your Own   Use what you know about the text and your own experience.

1. Think of other names for . . .

   a. the ship. _____

   _____

   b. the book. _____

   _____

2. Draw and label where you think Captain Fishhook might find the buried treasure.

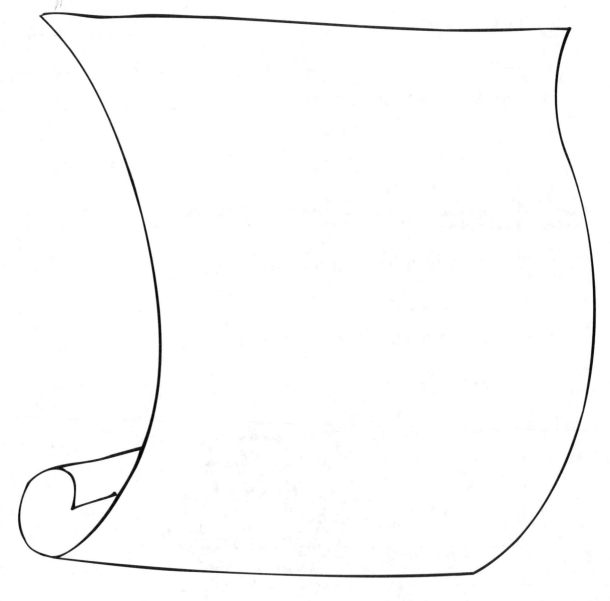

CAPTAIN FISHHOOK AND THE BURIED TREASURE

Making Connections

After reading the text on page 80, complete the following by making the connection between what you already know and the new information from the text.

1. Make a book cover of your own in the space below. It can be a story you have read or one you make up. Check off the boxes when you put in all the different parts.

☐ book title   ☐ cover illustration   ☐ name of author   ☐ name of illustrator

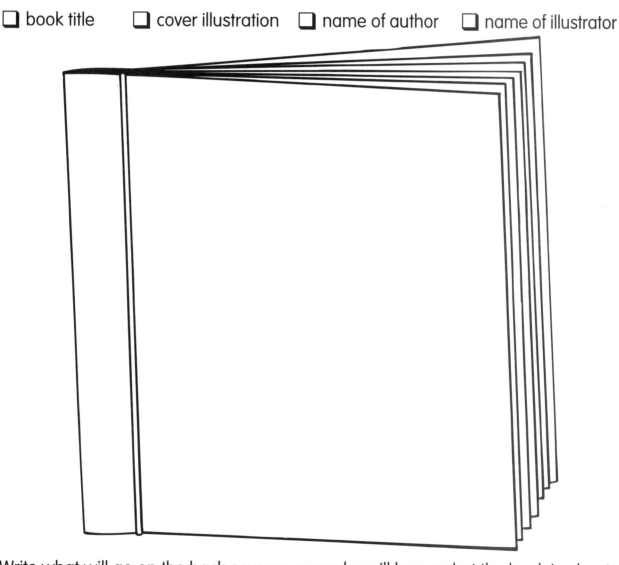

2. Write what will go on the back cover so a reader will know what the book is about.

_____

_____

_____

Genre: Myth

READING FOCUS

- Analyzes and extracts information from a myth to answer literal, inferential, and applied questions
- Uses synthesis to recall information and order details to sequence a story

ANSWER KEY

Right There (Page 86)

1. a. Zeus
   b. at the top of Mount Olympus
   c. on a gold throne
2. honeybee, deer, eagle, peacock
3. a. Zeus, wish   b. think   c. surprised
4. a. antlers
   b. a beautiful, colorful tail
   c. great wings
   d. the power to give great pain

Think and Search (Page 86)

1–3. Answers will vary.

On Your Own (Page 87)

Drawings and answers will vary.

Applying Strategies (Page 88)

1. One day, while sitting on his golden throne, Zeus had an idea.
2. The eagle wished for great wings so she could soar high.
3. The deer wished for antlers so he could use them against enemies.
4. The peacock wished for a beautiful, colorful tail.
5. The honeybee wished for the power to give any creature pain.
6. Answers/Drawings will vary.

EXTENSIONS

- Books containing myths suitable for this age group include the following:
  - *Greek Myths for Young Children* by Heather Amery
  - *15 Greek Myth Mini-Books* by Danielle Blood
  - *Classic Myths to Read Aloud* by William F. Russell

Name _____

Read the myth and answer the questions on the following pages.

Long ago, there was a king named Zeus. He lived at the top of Mount Olympus, where he could see all his kingdom. One day, while he was sitting on his gold throne, he had an idea. Instead of just giving gifts to people, he decided to give them to the animals as well.

He called the animals to gather around his gold throne. "Each of you will be granted one wish," said the king, "so think carefully."

The eagle wished for great wings so she could soar high in the sky. The deer wished for antlers so he could use them against enemies. The peacock wished for a beautiful, colorful tail. Then it was the honeybee's turn.

"What do you wish for, little honeybee?" asked the king.

"Only one wish will do," replied the honeybee. "I wish to have the power to give any creature great pain whenever I choose."

Zeus was surprised. "What a horrible wish, but I must grant it," said the king. "I will give you a sharp sting. However, you must only use it in times of anger or danger. And you will only be able to use it once, for using it will cost you your life."

And to this day, the little honeybee dies after it stings another creature.

THE HONEYBEE'S STING

| **Right There** | Find the answers directly in the text. |

1. Answer the questions.

   a. What was the king's name? _____

   b. Where did he live? _____

   c. Where did the king sit? _____

2. Place an **X** in the boxes next to the animals you read about in the story.

   ❑ honeybee   ❑ bear   ❑ deer   ❑ ant   ❑ eagle   ❑ peacock

3. Choose words from the word bank to complete each sentence.

| think   wish   surprised   Zeus |

   a. _____ granted each animal one _____.

   b. He told the animals to _____ carefully.

   c. Zeus was _____ when he heard the honeybee's wish.

4. Match each animal to what they wished for.

   a. deer   • great wings

   b. peacock   • antlers

   c. eagle   • the power to give great pain

   d. honeybee   • a beautiful, colorful tail

| **Think and Search** | Think about what the text says. |

Read each sentence and make a prediction. Choose **True** or **False**.

   1. Zeus was a kind king.   ❑ True ❑ False

   2. Zeus was a mean king.   ❑ True ❑ False

   3. Zeus was a wise king.   ❑ True ❑ False

THE HONEYBEE'S STING

Imagine Zeus has granted you one wish. Draw and write about what you would wish for.

_____

_____

_____

_____

_____

THE HONEYBEE'S STING

Use the text on page 85 to complete the activity. Draw the missing pictures and write the missing sentences. In the last box, draw and write what you think will happen next. Color and cut them out and put them in the correct order. Two have been numbered for you.

The eagle wished for great wings so she could soar high.

The honeybee wished for the power to give any creature pain.

Genre: Suspense

READING FOCUS

- Analyzes and extracts information from a suspense story to answer literal, inferential, and applied questions
- Predicts, using prior knowledge and information provided in the text
- Summarizes the story within a given framework

ANSWER KEY

Right There (Page 91)

1. a. cup
   b. book
   c. on a piece of paper
   d. snails

2. Three of the following: noisy, messy, little pest, little rascal.

Think and Search (Page 91)

1. a. Yes   b. No   c. No   d. No   e. Yes

2. Hannah has looked after her brother on more than one occassion.

On Your Own (Page 92)

Drawings and answers will vary.

Applying Strategies (Page 93)

- Hannah was reading a magic book.
- Her mother went next door to have coffee with the neighbor.
- Her little brother was being a bother.
- She wrote magic words, and she drew a picture of a snail next to her brother's name.
- Then she said the magic spell out loud.
- She couldn't hear what her brother was up to.
- She went to check on him.
- Then Hannah noticed the snails in the back yard.
- Hannah yelled for her mom.

EXTENSIONS

- The class can brainstorm some of the comments Hannah's mother may have made when Hannah told her what had happened. These can be written on the board using speech bubbles.
- Students can read other stories about people or things being changed by magic, including the following:
  - "Cinderella"
  - "The Frog Prince"
  - "Rumplestiltskin"

Name _____

Read the suspense story and answer the questions on the following pages.

Hannah was reading an interesting book about magic. She read about lots of tricks you could play on your family and friends. One part was all about making things disappear, and another one was about making things change.

Her mom had gone next door for a cup of coffee with Mrs. White, and Hannah had to look after her little brother again. He really was a noisy, messy, little pest who just kept getting in the way and driving her nuts. He was playing some loud, boring computer game and yelling and shouting. She decided to try out one of the magic tricks.

On a piece of paper, she copied the words of one of the magic spells and wrote her brother's name beside it. Next to it she drew a picture of a big, fat snail. She held on to the paper and started to read out the words. The wind picked up and before she had finished, the wind blew the paper away, so she had to make up the last bit.

Her brother was very quiet, and she wondered what trouble he was getting into this time. She went in to see, but he wasn't in the computer room. "Where is the little rascal?" she asked herself as she walked around the house, but he was nowhere to be seen.

Hannah looked outside and noticed that there were a number of snails in the back yard. Just then she realized . . .

"Mom, Mom, Mom!" she screamed.

THE MAGIC TRICK

Right There   Find the answers directly in the text.

1. Write the missing words from the story.

   a. Hannah's mother was having a _____ of coffee.

   b. The _____ was about magic tricks.

   c. Hannah wrote the magic words on _____.

   d. Hannah noticed a number of _____ in the back yard.

2. List three descriptions the author shared about Hannah's little brother.

   - _____

   - _____

   - _____

Think and Search   Think about what the text says.

1. Read each sentence. Choose **Yes** or **No**.

   a. Hannah enjoyed reading.   ❑ Yes ❑ No

   b. All the words Hannah read out were written   ❑ Yes ❑ No
   in the book.

   c. Hannah wasn't worried about what her little   ❑ Yes ❑ No
   brother was getting into.

   d. Her little brother was fun to look after.   ❑ Yes ❑ No

   e. Hannah was panicked.   ❑ Yes ❑ No

2. How do you know that Hannah's mom trusted her
   to watch her brother?

   _____

   _____

   _____

THE MAGIC TRICK

On Your Own   Use what you know about the text and your own experience.

What happened to Hannah's little brother? Draw a picture and write a sentence telling what you think really happened to him.

_____

_____

_____

_____

THE MAGIC TRICK

Paraphrasing/ Summarizing

Use the story on page 90 to complete the following activity. Tell the story again in your own words.

Hannah was reading	Her mother
Her little brother was	She wrote magic words, and she drew
Then she said the	She couldn't hear
So she went	Then Hannah noticed
Hannah yelled	

Teacher Information

READING FOCUS

- Analyzes and extracts information from a fairy tale to answer literal, inferential, and applied questions
- Makes predictions about specific characters
- Synthesizes information to comprehend and sequence events

ANSWER KEY

Right There (Page 96)

1. Yes	2. No	3. No	4. Yes	5. Yes

Think and Search (Page 96)

1. The king didn't think she looked like a princess because she was a mess.
2. Answers will vary.
3. It was a test to see if she was a real princess.
4. She slept on the pea.

On Your Own (Page 97)

Answers/Drawings will vary.

Applying Strategies (Page 98)

1. a. 5	b. 4	c. 1	d. 6	e. 3	f. 2

2. Check drawings for accuracy to see if it matches the sequence from question #1.

EXTENSIONS

- Students can dramatize particular scenes from the fairy tale.
- Other fairy tales involving princesses include the following:
    - "Sleeping Beauty"
    - "Snow White"
    - "The Twelve Dancing Princesses"
    - "The Frog Prince"
- Students can discuss similarities and differences between modern and fairy-tale princesses.

Name _____

Read the fairy tale and answer the questions on the following pages.

Once upon a time, there was a prince who wanted to marry a real princess. He traveled the world and met many girls who said they were princesses, but there was something about each one that wasn't quite right. He went home feeling very discouraged.

One evening, there was a terrible storm. The wind was roaring, and rain was pouring down. The king heard knocking at the castle gates. He found a young girl there who said she was a princess and asked for his help. She didn't look like a princess. She had water dripping from her hair, her clothes were soaked, and her shoes were full of water. The king didn't believe her, but he told her that she could stay for one night.

"We'll soon find out if she is a real princess," said the wise old queen.

She said nothing, but she took everything off the bed and placed a tiny pea on it. On top, she placed 20 mattresses and 20 quilts. Only a true, delicate princess would be able to tell the difference.

The next morning, when they asked the girl how she had slept, she replied, "Very badly. I don't know what it was, but I was lying on something hard, and this morning I am black-and-blue."

The prince and his family were very pleased. He took her for his wife, and they all lived happily ever after.

THE PRINCESS AND THE PEA

Right There   Find the answers directly in the text.

Read each sentence. Choose **Yes** or **No**.

1. The girl could feel the pea in her bed.   ❏ Yes   ❏ No

2. The queen told the king what she was
going to do.   ❏ Yes   ❏ No

3. The girl had a good night's sleep.   ❏ Yes   ❏ No

4. This story has a happy ending.   ❏ Yes   ❏ No

5. The prince went on a long trip, looking
for a princess.   ❏ Yes   ❏ No

Think and Search   Think about what the text says.

1. Why didn't the king think the girl was a real princess?

_____

_____

2. Do you think the king was a kind man?   ❏ Yes   ❏ No

Why or why not? _____

_____

3. Why didn't the queen tell anyone about the pea?

_____

_____

4. Why was the princess black-and-blue?

_____

_____

THE PRINCESS AND THE PEA

On Your Own   Use what you know about the text and your own experience.

Pretend you were the queen. Draw and write about another way you could test to see if the young girl was a real princess.

_____

_____

_____

_____

THE PRINCESS AND THE PEA

Sequencing

Use the story on page 95 to complete this activity.

1. Write the numbers 1–6 next to each sentence to show the order of events that took place in the story.

a. _____ The girl wakes up after a bad night's sleep.

b. _____ The queen puts a pea in the bed.

c. _____ The prince goes traveling, looking for a princess.

d. _____ The prince and princess get married.

e. _____ The girl knocks on the castle door.

f. _____ The prince comes home without a princess.

2. Draw pictures to show the order in which things happened in the story.

1	2	3
4	**5**	**6**

Genre: Adventure

READING FOCUS

- Analyzes and extracts information from an adventure story to answer literal, inferential, and applied questions
- Scans text to seek specific information to provide answers
- Uses synthesis to offer possible answers to divergent questions

---

ANSWER KEY

Right There (Page 101)

1. a. False   b. True   c. False   d. True

2. Sam waved his arms wildly above his head.

Think and Search (Page 101)

1. Answers will vary. Possible answer(s): They were busy building a sandcastle together.

2. He was comforting Jess and told her not to worry.

3. Her eyes filled with tears.

4. Lifeguards rescued them.

On Your Own (Page 102)

1. Answers will vary. Possible answer(s): play near a lifeguard tower, be aware of the changing tides, wear plenty of sunscreen, drink plenty of water.

2. Drawings should correlate to the list from question #1.

Applying Strategies (Page 103)

1–6. Answers will vary.

EXTENSIONS

- Arrange a visit from local lifeguards to discuss beach or pool safety.
- The class can research coastal wildlife.
- The class can compile a list of other community helpers.

STRANDED!

Name _____

Read the adventure story and answer the questions on the following pages.

Sam and Jess were digging a moat around their sandcastle. It had taken all morning to build their castle, and they were very proud of it. Sam stood up and watched the sea rushing in to fill the moat. It added the final touch to their masterpiece.

Jess stopped suddenly and cried, "Sam, we're stranded! The sea has cut us off from the main beach! What shall we do?"

The friends looked at each other in dismay. They did not understand what had happened.

"My water bottle is empty," whispered Jess. Her eyes filled with tears. "I can feel my skin prickling, too. I need some more sunscreen."

"Don't worry, Jess, I'll look after you," comforted Sam.

He put his arm around his young friend. He had no idea what to do. Suddenly, a bright orange flash in the water caught his eye.

"Over here!" he shouted.

He ran to the water's edge, waving his arms wildly above his head. Within minutes, Sam and Jess were on board the life raft, enjoying their ride back to the main beach.

STRANDED!

| **Right There** | Find the answers directly in the text. |

1. Read each sentence. Decide if each statement is **True** or **False**.

   a. Sam and Jess were building a volcano.   ☐ True ☐ False

   b. Jess had no water left.   ☐ True ☐ False

   c. They were at the beach in the evening.   ☐ True ☐ False

   d. The life raft was orange.   ☐ True ☐ False

2. What did Sam do to attract the attention of the lifeguards?

_____

_____

| **Think and Search** | Think about what the text says. |

1. Sam and Jess enjoyed their morning at the beach. Say why you think this statement is true.

_____

_____

_____

2. How can you tell that Sam is a kind person?

_____

_____

3. Which sentence in the story tells us that Jess was upset?

_____

_____

4. Who rescued Sam and Jess?

_____

STRANDED!

On Your Own   Use what you know about the text and your own experience.

1. Name three things you can do to make playing on the beach safer.

   • _____

   • _____

   • _____

2. Use your list to draw a "Safety at the Beach" poster.

STRANDED!

Use the text on page 100 to answer the questions. Think about the questions below. What do you think the answers might be? There are no right or wrong answers.

1. How old are Sam and Jess?

_____

2. Why are Sam and Jess at the beach together?

_____

_____

_____

3. Where are their parents?

_____

_____

4. Why did they build their sandcastle away from the main beach?

_____

_____

_____

5. Who was waiting for Sam and Jess back at the main beach?

_____

_____

_____

6. What was said to Sam and Jess about their adventure?

_____

_____

_____

Genre: Report

READING FOCUS

- Analyzes and extracts information from a report to answer literal, inferential, and applied questions
- Scans text to determine important information
- Summarizes text by recording keywords and phrases

ANSWER KEY

Right There (Page 106)

1. a. North   b. thick, hair   c. four, sharp, paws

2. The polar bear has lots of little bumps on the bottom of its paws to help its grip on the ice.

3. a. True   b. False   c. False   d. True   e. False

Think and Search (Page 106)

1. cub

2. Answers will vary.

On Your Own (Page 107)

1. eagle, tiger, lion

2. Drawings will vary.

Applying Strategies (Page 108)

1. North Pole

2. coat—very thick, white
   legs—strong, four
   claws—sharp
   teeth—sharp
   paws—large with little bumps on the bottom

3. seals

4. Answers will vary.

5. Drawings will vary.

EXTENSIONS

- Students may enjoy reading books about animal facts from the following series, before writing a simple report for others to read:
  - *Animal Books for Young Children* published by Acorn Naturalists
  - *The Faces of Nature Series* by Mymi Doinet
  - *Wild, Wild World Series* by Tanya Lee Stone

Name _____

Read the report and answer the questions on the following pages.

The polar bear is the largest bear in the world. It lives along the shores, on the ice, and in the ice-cold Arctic Ocean near the North Pole.

The polar bear has a very thick white coat of hair that helps to keep it warm. It walks on four strong legs and has sharp claws on its very large paws. The paws have lots of little bumps on the bottom to help its grip on the ice. The polar bear has sharp teeth to help it eat its food.

The polar bear is usually found living alone, but a polar bear cub will live with its mother for about two and a half years. She protects it and teaches it how to hunt for food.

The polar bear hunts seals as its main food. It finds a seal's breathing hole in the ice. When the seal comes to the surface for a breath of air, the polar bear uses its huge paws and sharp claws to flip the seal up onto the ice.

A polar bear in the wild can live for about 20 years. One polar bear in a zoo lived for 41 years!

THE POLAR BEAR

Right There   Find the answers directly in the text.

1. Write words from the report to finish the sentences.

    a. The polar bear lives near the _____ Pole.

    b. It has a very _____ white coat of _____ .

    c. The polar bear has _____ strong legs, _____

    claws, and very large _____ .

2. What does the polar bear have on its paws to help its grip on the ice?

_____

_____

3. Read each sentence. Decide if each statement is **True** or **False**.

    a. The polar bear is the largest bear in the world.   ❏ True   ❏ False

    b. It lives in a warm place.   ❏ True   ❏ False

    c. It usually lives in a group.   ❏ True   ❏ False

    d. It can live for about 20 years in the wild.   ❏ True   ❏ False

    e. Its favorite food is fish.   ❏ True   ❏ False

Think and Search   Think about what the text says.

1. What is a young polar bear called? _____

2. Do you think a mother polar bear is kind?   ❏ Yes   ❏ No

Why or why not? _____

_____

THE POLAR BEAR

On Your Own   Use what you know about the text and your own experience.

1. Place an **X** next to the animals that have sharp claws like the polar bear.

   ❑ spider   ❑ eagle   ❑ tiger   ❑ mouse   ❑ elephant   ❑ lion

2. Draw and label two animals that have a very thick coat of hair like the polar bear.

_____

_____

THE POLAR BEAR

Use the text on page 105 to answer the questions. Write words and phrases from the report about the polar bear to complete the chart.

The Polar Bear

1. Where does it live? _____

2. Write words to say what it looks like.

coat	legs

claws	teeth

paws

3. What does it mainly eat? _____

4. Interesting fact _____

5. Draw a polar bear near the seal's breathing hole.

Standards Correlations

Each lesson meets one or more of the following Common Core State Standards © Copyright 2010. National Governors Association Center for Best Practices and Council of Chief State School Officers. All rights reserved. For more information about the Common Core State Standards, go to *http://www.corestandards.org/* or *http://www.teachercreated.com/standards.*

Reading Literature/Fiction Text Standards	Text Title	Pages
Key Ideas and Details		
ELA.RL.2.1 Ask and answer such questions as *who, what, where, when, why,* and *how* to demonstrate understanding of key details in a text.	Adam's New Friend Lost The Tin Trunk The Stork and the Fox The Little Creatures Johnny Appleseed A Visit from Planet Zog Monkey Business at the Zoo A Girl Named Bree The Honeybee's Sting The Magic Trick The Princess and the Pea Stranded!	9–13 14–18 19–23 24–28 29–33 49–53 54–58 64–68 74–78 84–88 89–93 94–98 99–103
ELA.RL.2.2 Recount stories, including fables and folktales from diverse cultures, and determine their central message, lesson, or moral.	The Stork and the Fox The Little Creatures Johnny Appleseed Monkey Business at the Zoo The Honeybee's Sting The Princess and the Pea Stranded!	24–28 29–33 49–53 64–68 84–88 94–98 99–103
ELA.RL.2.3 Describe how characters in a story respond to major events and challenges.	Adam's New Friend Lost The Tin Trunk The Stork and the Fox The Little Creatures Johnny Appleseed A Visit from Planet Zog Monkey Business at the Zoo The Honeybee's Sting The Princess and the Pea Stranded!	9–13 14–18 19–23 24–28 29–33 49–53 54–58 64–68 84–88 94–98 99–103

Reading Literature/Fiction Text Standards *(cont.)*	Text Title	Pages
Craft and Structure		
ELA.RL.2.4 Describe how words and phrases (e.g., regular beats, alliteration, rhymes, repeated lines) supply rhythm and meaning in a story, poem, or song.	Lost A Visit from Planet Zog A Girl Named Bree	14–18 54–58 74–78
ELA.RL.2.5 Describe the overall structure of a story, including describing how the beginning introduces the story and the ending concludes the action.	The Honeybee's Sting The Magic Trick The Princess and the Pea Stranded!	84–88 89–93 94–98 99–103
ELA.RL.2.6 Acknowledge differences in the points of view of characters, including by speaking in a different voice for each character when reading dialogue aloud.	The Tin Trunk Johnny Appleseed Monkey Business at the Zoo The Honeybee's Sting	19–23 49–53 64–68 84–88
Integration of Knowledge and Ideas		
ELA.RL.2.7 Use information gained from the illustrations and words in a print or digital text to demonstrate understanding of its characters, setting, or plot.	Adam's New Friend The Tin Trunk The Stork and the Fox The Little Creatures A Visit from Planet Zog The Honeybee's Sting The Princess and the Pea	9–13 19–23 24–28 29–33 54–58 84–88 94–98
Range of Reading and Level of Text Complexity		
ELA.RL.2.10 By the end of the year, read and comprehend literature, including stories and poetry, in the grades 2–3 text complexity band proficiently, with scaffolding as needed at the high end of the range.	Adam's New Friend Lost The Tin Trunk The Stork and the Fox The Little Creatures Johnny Appleseed A Visit from Planet Zog Monkey Business at the Zoo A Girl Named Bree The Honeybee's Sting The Magic Trick The Princess and the Pea Stranded!	9–13 14–18 19–23 24–28 29–33 49–53 54–58 64–68 74–78 84–88 89–93 94–98 99–103